1726

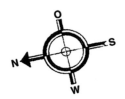

1744–1746

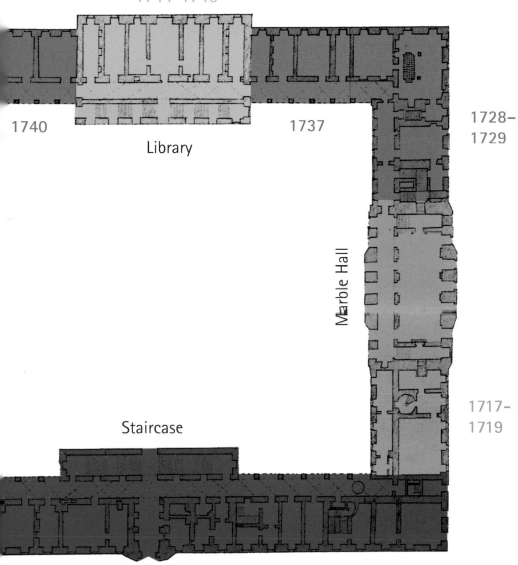

1740

1737

1728–
1729

Library

Marble Hall

1717–
1719

Staircase

95–1712

Entrance Portal

Prelacy

Augustinian Collegiate Foundation St. Florian

Johann Holzinger
Friedrich Buchmayr (ed.)

Photos by
Constantin Beyer

Translation by
Joseph Swann

SCHNELL + STEINER

Illustrations
Pages 2, 14, 16, 33, 40 bottom, inside
front and back covers, Augustinian
Collegiate Foundation, St. Florian;
all other photographs, Constantin Beyer,
Weimar

Bibliographic information published by the Deutsche Nationalbibliothek The Deutsche Nationalbibliothek lists this publication in the Deutsche Nationalbibliografie; detailed bibliographic data are available on the Internet at http://dnb.dnb.de .

First English Edition 2015
ISBN: 978-3-7954-2935-5
This publication is no. 239 of our "Große Kunstführer" series, founded by Dr. Hugo Schnell † and Dr. Johannes Steiner †.

© 2015 Verlag Schnell & Steiner GmbH,
Leibnizstr. 13, 93055 Regensburg,
Germany
Tel. +49-941 7 87 85-0
Fax +49-941 7 87 85-16
Printed by Erhardi Druck GmbH,
Regensburg

For further information about our
publishing programme visit
www.schnell-und-steiner.de

Front cover:
View of the basilica from the south-west

Back cover:
View of the foundation from the east with
the library and summer refectory annexe

Inside front cover:
Ground plan of the foundation with
building dates

Inside back cover:
Ground plan of the basilica

Contents

Welcome to the Collegiate Foundation of St. Florian

View of St. Florian's
from the south-east

You are most welcome here. Even in a rich historical region like Upper Austria, St. Florian's is unique. There is no centre of Christian culture quite like it. Not many places can boast a history that reaches back continuously more than 1700 years.

I hope you enjoy your visit – that you will have time to walk the long corridors of our buildings. Doing so should bring you inner peace. In the basilica you will have a moment to pause and think, to steep yourself in silence or listen to the sounds of the Bruckner organ. The magnificent architecture will do its part to lift your spirits, so that your heart and mind can find joy in all the beauty that has been created and assembled here over the centuries.

The Collegiate Foundation of St. Florian is first and foremost a place for seeking contact with God, a place of prayer and pilgrimage. We as Augustinian canons are called to pursue that aim. It is our wish that everyone who comes here should feel strengthened and renewed when they leave. Take in the breadth of our house and our landscapes. Breathe the deeper joy and tranquillity that comes from faith in him to whose glory all this has been created.

+ Johann Holzinger
Provost

St. Florian and the origins of the foundation

By the turn of the 4th century CE, Christianity already had numerous adherents in the Roman province of Ufernoricum. Among them was Florianus, the highest administrative official in the province. He was already living in retirement in the town of Cetium (St. Pölten) when in 304 a rigorous persecution of Christians decreed by the Emperor Diocletian reached the outer limits of the empire. There, in Cetium, Florianus (or Florian as he was later known) learned that a considerable number of Christians had been taken prisoner in Lauriacum (Enns-Lorch), the town where he had formerly held office. Feeling it was his duty to take his stand as a Christian, and to encourage his co-religionists in their faith, Florian went immediately to Lauriacum. His courageous appearance before the provincial governor did not save him, however, from execution, and on **May 4, 304** he was drowned in the River Enns.

No later event of this or any similar kind occurred to dim the memory of the Lorch martyrs, and the honour accorded to these last witnesses of the early church soon stood on an equal footing with the veneration of the Christian proto-martyrs. In the Middle Ages this found palpable expression in the formal burial of St. Florian between Sts. Stephen and Laurence in the church of St. Laurence Outside the Walls in Rome, from where, towards the end of the 12th century, a Polish delegation is said to have taken his relics to Cracow.

Pride in the fact that Florian belonged to the provincial upper class contributed to the fact that he was not forgotten. His memory was also kept alive, however, by a short report of his martyrdom, the *Passio Floriani*, written by an unknown author who was still clearly well informed about the political and legal situation in the 4th century Roman Empire: the report contains details no later hagiographer could have known. In fact the town of Cetium, where Florian had lived as a retired official, soon fell into a centuries-long oblivion.

The people of the region had always treated the **grave of St. Florian** – situated near a group of beech trees, probably in the grounds of an ancient Roman villa rustica – as a place of pil-

St. Florian as a knight – wood carving by a Moravian master (c. 1320)

Provost Leonhard
Riesenschmied before
St.Florian, by the
master of the
St. Florian Crucifixion
Triptych (c. 1480–90)

grimage; and in the early 8th century, when organized ecclesiastical structures began to take root in the territories of the Bavarii, a notable cultic centre may have been established at this time-honoured site of Christian devotion. Infused with a pure theological spirit, the veneration of the saint flourished without relics or even a visible grave. No spectacular cache of relics was reported, nor was there ever talk of a single personality as founder of the shrine. On the contrary, it was always held that the local people were themselves the founders. At no point did the bishops of Passau claim to have established a religious community there.

In the 8th century the brief *Passio Floriani* from the 4th century was extended, again by an unknown hand. The readership to whom it was directed can, however, only have been local or regional. Every saint, and especially a martyr who had always been highly honoured, was accorded special powers of mediation, whose plausibility was best anchored in tales of miracles. But this longer version of the saint's martyrdom contains remarkably few concrete examples of such happenings. Its compiler seems to have been more interested in general reference to the miracles of Jesus as described in the Bible.

St. Florian, the brave confessor of the faith who gave his own life in the Christian cause, became in due course the patron saint of a good death, and later, when persecution ceased, the stalwart defender of Christian lands against any who threatened them and their faith from without. Finally, from the 15th century, he was venerated as the special protector against the danger of fire and flood.

From the early 9th century the number of written references to a community at the shrine of St. Florian increases, among them a remarkable annotation by a scribe from Regensburg, stating that he had finished copying a book at St. Florian's (monastery) on September 12, 819 – almost 1200 years ago. He obviously took for granted that his contemporaries would be familiar with this place of pilgrimage. That St. Florian's was an independent foundation in the diocese of Passau was known in Frankfurt in 823. In 901 St. Florian's is mentioned in defence plans against the Hungarians, and a century later, only a few days after his election, King Henry II signed a decree (dated July 20, 1002) putting the foundation on a securer economic footing.

In the wake of the great 11th century church reform, the monastic community, which had so far lived in accordance with the Canonical Rule of Aachen (816), was in 1071 incorporated by Bishop Altmann of Passau into the order of Augustinian Canons. In subsequent decades the priests of St. Florian's assumed pastoral duties in parts of Upper and Lower Austria, giving rise to a network of more than 30 incorporated parishes.

Karl Rehberger

Architectural history of the foundation

◼ Medieval beginnings

The oldest written document referring to the physical buildings of St. Florian's is the deed of foundation of the community of Augustinian Canons by Bishop Altmann of Passau in 1071. It is recorded that on this occasion the bishop consecrated a church with five altars, which had been rebuilt on the site of an earlier (pre-955) church destroyed by the Hungarians. The new church burned down in 1235; the nave was then rebuilt and a vaulted choir added, but the vault collapsed in 1250 when nearing completion. Remnants of the crypt of this polygonal choir are still preserved beneath the choir of the present Baroque church. After this disaster a fresh start was made around 1275, and in 1291 the **new collegiate church** – an early Gothic three-aisled basilica with vaulted ceiling – was consecrated. At the beginning of the 14th century a massive bell tower was erected at the western corner of the south aisle. The lower and middle section of this tower form part of the south tower of the present Baroque church.

Nothing is known of the history or appearance of the medieval collegiate buildings, but a copperplate engrav-

The medieval / early
Baroque foundation
from the south (1674)
– copperplate
engraving by Matthäus
Vischer

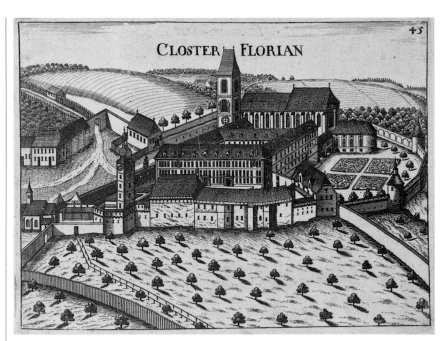

ing in *Matthäus Vischer's* Topography of Upper Austria (1674) shows the late Gothic collegiate buildings, which included a defensive entrance gate and tower and, stretching eastward, a number of service and administrative buildings, ending with the provost's residence.

the other buildings of this period fell victim to the high Baroque wave of reconstruction, even the sacristy added in 1652 to the east of the church choir, which – as can be seen in Vischer's copperplate print of 1674 – was substantial and architecturally imposing.

Early Baroque period

Between 1628 and 1630 Provost Leopold Zehetner replaced the medieval collegiate buildings almost entirely with a uniform three-storey construction in the sober style of the age. At the same time the Gothic church was given a Baroque refit under the supervision of the Linz master-builder *Markus Martin Spaz,* who came from a family of Italian builders. Still largely preserved, the south wing of this phase of construction, containing offices, guestrooms and prelacy apartments, now constitutes the north wing of the main courtyard group. The name **Leopold Wing** commemorates its initiator. All

High Baroque reconstruction

Set in motion by Provost David Fuhrmann, the high Baroque development of the foundation began slowly (and outside the foundation proper) with the construction in 1674–76, probably by *Francesco Canevale*, of the Meierhof or dairy (now a fire service museum) to the west of the main complex. Arranged around four sides of a large inner courtyard, this impressive building was extended before 1685 by the addition of a further three wings. Canevale probably also rebuilt the Johannesspital (St. John's Hospital) on the town market place

9

DAVID FUHRMANN PRÆPOSITUS. XXXVII. ELECTUS. 1667.
SEDIT ANNOS 22. OBIJT. 1689. ÆTAT: 67.

Provost David
Fuhrmann, 1753 –
portrait from the
Prelates' Gallery by
Johann Georg Tompke

(1677–1680). This was followed in 1681–1683 by the construction in the Hofgarten (today the collegiate gardens) to the south-west of the main complex of a delightful pavilion, for whose planning *Carlo Antonio Carlone* would have been responsible. A well-known master-builder from northern Italy, Carlone is also thought

to have directed the Baroque refurbishment of the Johannesspital Church in 1681. He was probably also the chosen architect for a second, more thorough, Baroque refit planned for the Gothic collegiate foundation church, of which we know only that a monumental marble high altar was commissioned in 1682.

But at that point everything changed. Victory in the Battle of Kahlenberg in 1683 freed Austria from the Turkish threat and led to a mood of exultation throughout the country. On the feast of St. Florian in 1684 Emperor Leopold I made a pilgrimage of thanksgiving, with the Empress, to the grave of Austria's martyr-patron and protector. This so highlighted the importance of the foundation that the provost resolved to extend his plans into a **grand renewal** of the collegiate church and buildings, for which Carlone was then engaged to draw up a comprehensive unified concept.

Building work on the new church began in 1685, but the entire project was to take three architects and five provosts some 60 years to complete. Provost David Fuhrmann lived only to see the new vault and dome erected over the church choir in 1689. The

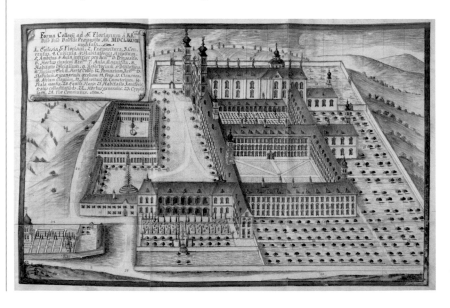

Copy of the rebuilding
project of 1685 – from
Topographia
Florianensis by Karl
Adam Heiss (1743)

nave, interior plasterwork and frescoes were completed under his successor, Matthäus von Weissenberg, between 1690 and 1695. The upper storeys of the two west façade towers took rather longer, being completed in 1700 and 1712 respectively.

Work on the collegiate buildings, set around the two smaller courtyards immediately south of the church and the large Prelates' Court beyond, started in 1695. The west wing, adjoining the south-west tower of the church, was almost complete by the time of Carlone's death in 1708. Apart from the Lady Chapel at its northernmost end, the west wing contains in hierarchical succession the collegiate offices, provost's apartments, guest rooms and imperial suite. Partly interconnected, the rooms open at all levels onto long corridors on the courtyard side. In harmony with the architectural ideals of the late 17th century, the exterior walls, with their unbroken lines of windows uniformly set between tall pilasters, also emphasize the great length of the building, which is free from any other projections. Carlone originally intended to set the festive hall of the foundation in a separate south-west annexe at the end of the west wing, but his successor, the renowned Austrian master-builder and monastery architect *Jakob Prandtauer*, dispensed with this addition. Instead, he completed the west front in 1712 with a powerful statement in the form of an imposing entrance portal to the main foundation group, and placed the festive hall at the centre of the future south wing of the Prelates' Court. In 1711 Prandtauer also undertook significant alterations to the open staircase planned by Carlone for the west wing of the Prelates' Court, endowing Provost Franz Claudius Kröll's prestigious project with the shape it still has today.

After completing the west wing, Prandtauer turned his attentions to the canons' apartments, which were built between 1714 and 1719. Running south from the choir of the church, parallel to the west wing, this unadorned section of the building joined the Leopold Wing – all that

11

was left from the early Baroque period of reconstruction – which now formed the north wing of the Prelates' Court. Before the canons' wing was finished, Provost Johann Baptist Födermayr, a lover of pomp, pressed forward with the construction of the south wing, beginning from the west. Working on two fronts, he was able to complete the shell of the Marble Pavilion in the same year as the canons' apartments (1719), though the interior of this magnificent building took many more years to finish.

Before the remaining gap in the quadrangle of the Prelates' Court could be closed, the most difficult technical problem of the entire project had to be

solved: preparing the eastern bank, which sloped steeply down to the market town of St. Florian, so that it could be built upon. Prandtauer attacked the problem from the north, evening out the north-south slope of the existing gardens, and building massive foundations on them to take the additional wing. On this substructure (which contains two cellar floors) he also built the summer refectory (begun in 1725), a virtually freestanding unit joined to the canons' quarters only by a low corridor. It was originally planned that this handsome flat-roofed building with its Attic cornice should receive a counterpart to the north and (later) another to the east, so that the canons could enjoy a secluded garden for their relaxation. But this part of the plan was not implemented.

After Prandtauer's death in 1726 *Jakob Steinhuber*, who for many years had been his site manager, continued the master's work, completing the eastern section, as well as the south-east corner, of the Prelates' Court on the newly constructed foundations in 1728-1729. However, before starting work on the library building, the provost decided to split the north quadrangle into two distinct courtyards by building a single-storey wing across it, joining two taller staircases at the northern and southern ends. This wing served initially as a so-called Komödienhaus for theatrical performances, but was later divided into separate rooms, which in 1770, when a second storey was added, were converted into guest apartments – a purpose this part of the building regained in 2005 after the most recent phase of lengthy refurbishment.

As a man of learning, Födermayr's successor, Provost Johann Georg Wiesmayr, took a personal interest in the completion of what he saw as the final glory of St. Florian's, the collegiate library. As was his nature, he went about the project with great

care, first finishing the substructure and cellars, and then in 1737 the south, and in 1740 the north section of the library wing. The only thing lacking was the centrepiece, whose two upper floors would house the great main room of the library. In 1744, however, when work was due to begin the provost decided to revise Prandtauer's plans, a task he entrusted to the experienced architect *Gotthard Hayberger* trom Steyr. Hay-berger immediately produced new plans, many aspects of which were, in fact, derived from Prandtauer. As a special precaution, fire walls were added to the roof space, and ceilings throughout the building were massively vaulted. The shell of the library was completed by 1746, but it took several years more to fit out the interior, with detailed work continuing even after 1750.

Thomas Korth

A community of priests in the spirit of St. Augustine

Since its earliest beginnings, the community at the grave of St. Florian has been a centre of spirituality devoted to pastoral work, not only in the immediate vicinity but also further afield. In 1071 Bishop Altmann of Passau established **Augustinian canons** at the church – an order of priests dedicated not purely to community life but also to pastoral care among the local people. Local, however, should be understood in the wider sense, for the incorporated parishes in which the canons pursue their work, far from forming a territorial unity, are spread across several districts of Upper Austria. Currently 33 in number, they represent no small task for the diminishing number of priests at St. Florian's.

Derived from **St. Augustine** (354–430), the guiding concept of such an eccle-

siastical institution demanded that pastoral care should be appropriate to the time in question: Augustine was a priest and bishop dedicated in every fibre of his being to the people of his day and their very diverse needs. He was also, however, concerned to give vital embodiment to the original impulse of the early church, of which the opening chapters of the Acts of the Apostles provided eloquent testimony. It is for this reason that he organized a form of priestly life that united the concepts of religious order and pastoral mission. The early Middle Ages took up the idea as attractive as well as effective, and implemented it in the Order of Canons Regular of St. Augustine, a body which became instrumental in many reform movements not only in France and Italy but also (indeed especially) in South Germany and Austria.

Around 400 CE Augustine wrote a text for the guidance of men and women living in a religious community. Known as the **Rule of St. Augustine**, it had an immense impact on the history of the spiritual life. Though he himself did not establish any religious order and was writing purely for the communities under his care, many later founders have been influenced by his rule. The initial impulse, to be "of one heart and soul" (Acts 4.32) on the way to God, should, he taught, always be recalled. An indispensable prerequisite for

such an attitude is to love and share: "they had everything in common. [...] There was not a needy person among them" (Acts 4.32–34). Augustine's rule, as the guiding spirit of the order, is notable for its psychological subtlety. "More prayer than prescription", it refrains from specific ascetic or spiritual directives, encouraging rather a consistently thoughtful, spiritual attitude based on all-embracing solidarity and readiness to forgive. At the end of the rule stands a principle that applies not only to the members of the order but to all who share a common faith – indeed to all who aspire to live together: "feel yourselves not as slaves under the law, but as free people under God's grace."

This intention informs the everyday life of the collegiate community with its daily Mass and threefold recitation of the office. Major feasts are celebrated with a solemn liturgy in the basilica and vespers chanted in the traditional Gregorian manner. Monthly days of recollection and annual retreats enable the canons to focus on the source of their religious commitment. Eating, talking and celebrating together, whether in small or larger groups, fosters the exchange of views and experience and verifies the words of the Psalmist: "Behold, how good and pleasant it is, when brothers dwell in unity!" (Ps 133). In particular, the discussion of questions of faith enables us – not only within our own walls but also in our pastoral work – to fulfil the spirit of St. Augustine and "always be prepared to make a defence to any one who calls you to account for the hope that is in you" (1 Pet. 3.15).

Ferdinand Reisinger

Collegiate Basilica of the Assumption

▆ Façade

Visitors to the basilica at St. Florian's generally enter through the Einsertor, the great main gate of the collegiate foundation. Walking the 204 m of the west front, with its long rows of windows protected on the first floor with fine wrought-iron gratings, and its regularly spaced vertical white pilasters, they pass at the halfway-point *Leonhard Sattler's* **entrance portal** (1712–13) to the Prelates' Court, surmounted by the Baroque roof-turret of the Bläserturm (Fanfare Tower). Supported by muscular Atlanteans, the balcony over the entrance doors is flanked by two pairs of figures representing the virtues of the foundation's chief patron St. Florian (fortitude and courage), and the father of the Order of Canons, St. Augustine (faith and eloquence). Reaching the Lady Chapel windows, the visitor will instinctively look up at the 84 m high towers of the basilica, wondering perhaps why it is necessary to traverse the entire length of the collegiate buildings before arriving at the church.

Inscribed in gold above the **church entrance** – again flanked by the figures of Sts. Florian and Augustine – are the words of the prophet Isaiah, "Laetificabo eos in domo orationis meae" ("I will make them joyful in my house of prayer", Is 56.7). The mood of the visitor entering this house should, then, be one of joy. The same visitor, however, may well be initially overwhelmed by the sheer dimensions of the church and the Baroque wealth of its ornamentation. Built between 1686 and 1709, the basilica is 77 m long and 36 m high to the crown of its central dome. It was the first church north of the Alps whose entire ceiling (4921 sq m) is covered with frescoes – works whose glowing colours contrast with the rich plasticity of the white wall mouldings. Architecture, painting, sculpture, wood-carving and ironwork complement each other here

Page 17:
West front of the
foundation with
basilica, entrance
portal and Bläserturm

Page 19:
View towards the high
altar of the basilica
from the porch, with
wrought-iron screen by
Hans Messner
(1698–99)

to create a magnificent artistic statement. All who take part in a solemn sung liturgy or attend a concert with music by Anton Bruckner – indeed all who simply enter the church to find a moment of spiritual peace – will experience something of that greater joy that opens behind the veil of sense perceptions.

Interior of the church

Separating the **porch** from the nave of the basilica is a finely executed wrought-iron screen (1698–1699),

the work of the Passau smith *Hans Messner*. Above it the eye is caught by the frescoes in the six-vaulted ceiling which – like all the other frescoes in the church – are by the Munich court painter *Johann Anton Gumpp* and his pupil *Melchior Steidl*. Inscribed at the centre of the first tripartite group is the divine response to King Solomon's prayer at the consecration of the Temple (2 Chron 7.14). The two paintings to the sides also remind supplicants that they can approach God in this holy place with confidence: on the left is the Return of the Prodigal Son

Page 21:
Interior of the basilica
looking east towards
the high altar

(Lk 15.18) and on the right the Repentant Tax Collector, of whom it is said "this man went down to his house justified" (Lk 18.14). The central image of the second vault shows Christ struggling with his Father's will in the Garden of Olives, while to the left Moses stands with outstretched hands supported in prayer, lest they fail during the battle with the Amalekites (Ex 17.11). Opposite Moses on the right is King David praying that the angel of war may sheathe the avenging sword (1 Chron 21.16). The frescoes remind the faithful that this is a place of prayer, harbouring the promise that whatever assails them will come to an end in the joy that awaits those who pray in hope.

Entering the **nave** through the iron-work screen, one is confronted in the broad central aisle of this house of God, not with a world that has no relation to life, but with a symbolic depiction of the Christian path, with its tribulations and final fulfilment. In this sense Prelate Wilhelm Neuwirth aptly described the basilica in 1996 as a "church of the way". This way is not a lonely trek – it is

Altar reredos, Chapel of St. Augustine, with painting by Johann Michael Rottmayr (1719)

Dome fresco –
Coronation of
the Virgin by
Johann Anton Gumpp
and Melchior Steidl

accompanied by tested travellers. Nor does it end in indeterminate nothingness, lost in fog or plunged in the abyss: it ends in the consummation of sharing in the divine fullness.

Dedicated to the saints, the **side chapels** demonstrate that the Christian way, though leading to death, has its final goal in eternal life. On the right one comes first to the Magdalen Altar, with a painting by *Andrea Celesti* (c. 1700). Opposite, in the Chapel of St. Barbara, is a painting by *Wenzel Halbax* (1694). The second pair of chapels, with altar paintings by *Michael Willmann* (1700), are (on the right) the Altar of the Guardian Angels, reminding the faithful that they are surrounded and

protected by beneficent powers, and (on the left) the Altar of St. Anne. The third pair consists of the Altar of St. Augustine, father of the Order of Canons Regular, with a strikingly colourful painting by *Johann Michael Rottmayr* (1719) (this chapel also contains the baptismal font and paschal candle, as the basilica serves at the same time as a parish church) and, facing it, the Altar of St. Florian, with the patron saint's martyrdom painted by *Leopold Schulz* (1848). The final pair of side altars approaching the choir remind the Christian that life is accompanied and sustained by the cross (Altar of the Crucifixion with a painting by the Vienna court artist *Peter Strudel*, 1698–99) and the mystery of God's humble presence in the Eucharist

Page 23:
Ceiling vault frescoes
in the nave by Johann
Anton Gumpp and
Melchior Steidl
(1690–1695)

22

Page 24:
High altar of the
basilica by Giovanni
Battista Colomba
(1682), with painting
of the Assumption of
the Virgin by
Giuseppe Ghezzi

(Chapel of the Last Supper with a painting by *Leopold Schulz*, 1848).

The **ceiling frescoes** in the five-vaulted nave are again by *Gumpp* and *Steidl*. They begin above the Bruckner organ with St. Cecilia as the patron of church music. The following four vaults depict different phases of St. Florian's martyrdom as an illustration of the Christian way. Accompanying the theme of the last two side chapels, the final fresco reminds the faithful that they too are called upon to bear the burden of the Cross but, strengthened by the Eucharist, may hope to be admitted, like St. Florian above them, into heaven.

The **pulpit** of black Lilienfeld marble (1755), by the Viennese court sculptor *Josef Ressler*, makes many references to the order's patron, St. Augustine, culminating in the figure of the learned bishop banishing error and heresy to the depths with his right hand, while his left, holding his burning heart, points up to the dome, with its fresco of the Coronation of the Virgin in Heaven. The front of the pulpit is decorated with a bas-relief of Augustine in the garden hearing the words "Take up [the book] and read" that triggered his conversion.

At the centre of the towering **high-altar reredos** (1682), created by *Giovanni Battista Colomba* in red Salzburg marble, is a depiction of the Assumption of the Blessed Virgin by *Giuseppe Ghezzi*. Mary's example should make palpably present that the Christian way is not one in which gifts simply fall from heaven with no readiness on the part of the recipient. The salvation that we can already joyfully anticipate presents itself only to those who are open to it. In this the Virgin Mary is our model: as it was with her, so it will be with us. To the left and right of the central painting stand four statues: the inner

two once again represent Sts. Florian and Augustine, the outer pair John the Baptist and St. Sebastian. The octagonal picture above portrays God the Father with Sts. Joseph and Leopold. Flanking it are statues of Sts. Catherine and Barbara. The topmost niche of the reredos contains the figure of King David, the name-patron of Provost David Fuhrmann who commissioned the altar. The designation of the Blessed Virgin as Tower of David in the Litany of Loreto suggests that the whole altar reredos could also be interpreted in a Marian sense.

Further Marian symbols – most of them also from the Litany of Loreto – can be found in the **choir vault frescoes**. In the centre foreground the curtain of the Solomonic Temple is drawn back to reveal the Ark of the Covenant, the Holy of Holies of the Old Testament people of God, now accessible to all mankind. The pendentives (cusps) of the vault feature four great Old Testament figures who, like Mary, foreshadowed human redemption: Noah with the ark, and the prophets Joel, Elijah and Isaiah. The four corners where the vault rests on the sill are devoted to the four evangelists – the cornerstones of the New Testament message.

The transepts of the church are merely hinted at in the somewhat recessed, or nately carved **choir stalls**, the work of the Linz sculptor *Adam Franz* (1702). The figures of the Church Fathers Augustine, Jerome, Gregory and Ambrose are by the Bolzano sculptor *Jakob Auer*. Here, too, the choir – the place where the Augustinian canons sing the divine office – must be seen in conjunction with the dome above, with its portrayal of the Coronation of the Virgin: an indication that the song of praise which is part and parcel of our lives will be taken up in heaven and perfected before God. Similarly, the

25

Page 26:
Pulpit by Josef Ressler
(1755), with choir stalls
by Adam Franz and
Jakob Auer and choir
organ by Josef Remmer
1691–92

fronts of the two choir organs, with the figures of the Angel Gabriel and the Mother of God, illustrate the dual character of the act of annunciation, for what is proclaimed must be heard and accepted. In this sense, too, the harmony of the organs' voices embodies that of the annunciation to Mary.

◼ Burial vault and crypt

Next to the Altar of the Crucifixion (front right) a door leads to the confessionals and sacristies, with steps descending to the crypt and burial vault. The first thing one sees in the antechamber to the **burial vault** is the large tombstone of Provost Peter Maurer (1522) with a remarkable relief of the crucifixion. The entrance to the vault itself is flanked by statues of Sts. Sebastian and Florian. Here, in the massive walls beneath the nave, 93 canons from the time before 1784 lie buried. Since that date, the canons have been buried in the priests' cemetery opposite the main entrance to the church. The side niches contain the coffins of provosts from the Baroque period and 20th century, alongside those of members of the Upper Austrian nobility. The Hapsburg Queen Catherine I of Poland (†1572) has a

Sarcophagus of the
composer Anton
Bruckner in the burial
vault below the main
organ loft

Page 29:
View from the nave to
the main organ by
Franz Xaver Krisman
(1770–1774)

chapel of her own. Against the back wall of the crypt are the bones from some 6000 graves of an early Christian cemetery, and on a plinth in front of them stands the pewter sarcophagus of Anton Bruckner, onetime basilica organist, who wished only to be buried immediately beneath 'his' organ.

The anteroom to the **crypt** contains portraits of the anchoress Wilbirg (†1291) and Bishop Altmann of Passau. Here, too, is the St. Florian chasuble which, with its metal collarpiece, was made by the Upper Austrian artist Maria Moser (b. 1948) for Collegiate Dean Ferdinand Reisinger, who wears it every year at the St. Florian's Day pilgrimage celebrations on May 4. The interior of the crypt is dominated by the mighty foundations of the Baroque marble high altar. Between them, remnants of late Romanesque windows and early Gothic rib vaulting can be seen. In fact, the memory of more than 1700 years of Austrian history is kept alive in this room, for here was the

first burial place of the martyr Florian, indicated symbolically by a millstone mounted on the wall. His civil courage and solidarity with the imprisoned and tortured Christians of Lorch is still remembered. Two stone sarcophagi hold the remains of Valeria, who oversaw the burial of St. Florian, and of the anchoress Wilbirg.

The visitor's journey has led from the Einsertor along the entire west façade of the main building back to the church. At St. Florian's one must go right back in order to arrive at the most central building, the house of God. This is the primordial place from which the more than 1700 year-long history of the foundation takes its origin. Beneath the high altar of the basilica the first saint of this country known by name, Florian of Noricum, was originally buried. Around the central altar – where Jesus Christ becomes present in the form of bread and wine in the sacred enactment – the faithful assemble, listen to their God, praise him, and receive his gifts of grace. From that centre flows the life that St. Florian's still sends out into the world. According to the inscription above its entrance, the basilica is there to bring joy and fruitfulness (for that, too, is the sense of the Latin word *laetificare*) to the people of this land, whose patron saint and protector is St. Florian.

Johann Holzinger

■ Organs

The two organs above the choir stalls were built in 1691–92 by *Josef Remmer* from Vienna. Renovated and altered several times, they have, since 1930, been electrically coupled and can be played from either of two consoles: one next to the choir stalls and the other on the south gallery.
In 1770 Provost Matthäus Gogl commissioned a new **main organ** for the

Crypt with sarcophagi
of Valeria (left) and the
anchoress Wilbirg
(†1289, right)

west gallery from the priest and organ builder *Franz Xaver Krismann* (1726–1795). The magnificent case, made by the master cabinetmaker *Johann Christian Jegg* from St. Florian, was finished by 1771, but the enormous instrument itself (74 registers, 59 stops, 3 manuals and pedals, 5230 pipes) was not ready until 1774, two years later than agreed. Because of technical problems (above all in the wind supply) further work became necessary over the following decades. In 1873–75 *Matthäus Mauracher* from Salzburg rebuilt and extended the instrument, and the four-manual console dating from this time can still be seen at Anton Bruckner's birthplace in Ansfelden. A second, more thorough refurbishment undertaken in 1930–32 included the installation of electric traction by *Mauracher Bros.* of Linz and *Dreher & Flamm* of Salzburg. But the renovated instrument (now 92 registers with 6159 pipes) was not destined to last long. In 1944 the Ottensheim firm of *Wilhelm Zika* was commissioned to rebuild it, and it re-entered service in 1951 with 103 registers, slider wind chest and electropneumatic traction. The latest restoration, completed in 1994–96 by the Upper Austrian organ builders *Kögler* of St. Florian, involved comprehensive technical renewal and the construction of four new registers. The instrument now has 7386 pipes, many of which – including the 32' principal at the front of the case – date from Krismann.

In 1747 the **Lady Chapel** received its own organ, built by *Nikolaus Rummel* from Linz. In 1911 Ignaz Bruckner, Anton Bruckner's brother – who among other functions at St. Florian's had been employed to tread the organ bellows – commissioned the present instrument from Maurachers'.

Klaus Sonnleitner

Prelates' sacristy

With plasterwork by *Franz Josef Holzinger* (from 1773) and frescoes by *Bartolomeo Altomonte* (1739), the architecture, art and furnishings of the **prelates' sacristy** – the foundation's principal room of its kind – form a unique harmony. Light and shade play intricately on the great central press for church vestments and hangings and the tall, elaborately inlaid cupboards that line the walls. The ceiling frescoes depict in turn the Eucharist as the embodiment of Christ the Paschal Lamb, the miracle of the manna in the desert (Ex 16.14), and Jesus' dialogue with the woman at Jacob's Well (Jn 4.7). The chalices, Mass vestments and other church equipment stored here, some of which stem from the 17th century, are used at divine services, adding variation and colour to the feasts of the liturgical year.

Bells

St. Florian's has a peal of 22 bells, plus the two hour-bells of the clock in the Bläserturm over the front entrance. The bells are, so to speak, the voice of the foundation, heard throughout the town and neighbourhood in some cases for centuries. The 11 historical bells, highly representative for any religious house, have in fact sounded for 400 years. Six of these bells are from the beginning of the 14th century. Of special interest are the paired bells of 1318 (Mary, F sharp, 1390 kg and Florian, A, 855 kg) and 1319 (Augustine, C sharp, 590 kg and Gregory, E, 350 kg). Other bells were added in 1471, 1648 (the Lady Bell cast by *Martin Fitler* in Linz, B, 3840 kg) and 1690. The largest bell in Upper Austria and a masterpiece of Baroque foundry work, the great north tower bell (F, 8845 kg, 245 cm in diameter) was cast by *Matthias Prininger* in Krems in 1717. The bell

cage, yoke and furnishings date from 1718. Installed in 2000, the youngest bell hangs in the south tower of the basilica.

An interesting counterbalance to the historical peal is the choir peal. Also installed in 2000, it consists of 10 small bells with a total weight of 1454 kg.

Harald Rüdiger Ehrl

Library

In the form of the east-wing library, the finishing touches were put to the Baroque rebuilding of the basilica and collegiate complex by the Steyr master-builder *Gotthard Hayberger* between 1744 and 1750. From the library roof *Johann Paul Sattler's* statues of the four virtues look down onto the Prelates' Court: (l. to r. on the outside) talent and zeal, (on the inside, somewhat elevated and thereby emphasized in importance) wisdom and awe. Provost Johann Georg Wiesmayr, who commissioned the library, sought to show in this ordering of gifts the godly dimension of all knowledge, beyond the reach of any mere human industry.

The **main room** (25 by 11 m) is lit by five tall east-facing windows (the central one a double window) and as many small upper windows concealed in deep niches. The splendid interior furnishings are the work of the cabinetmaker *Christian Jegg* and sculptor *Johann Paul Sattler*. The two-storey room lives from the many books that fill its shelves, as if to shelter the sphere of the mind from the outer world. Accessible only via a spiral staircase hidden behind a re-

volving door, an elegant gallery circles the room, seemingly suspended from the bookshelves, whose curving lines, emphasized by the galleried upper level, give this magnificent place of learning a delightful sense of movement.

The four Baroque cases in the centre of the room – like the main bookshelves richly decorated with inlay work – hold large-format maps. The two busts are of benefactors from the imperial household: Grand Duke Ferdinand of Tuscany (by *Johann Provost* 1805) and Archduke Charles (by *Leopold Kissling* 1817). The lunettes of the ceiling vault hold eight portraits of Greek sages and Roman rulers and six allegorical scenes interspersed with twelve allegories of learning. In the centre, above a tromp l'oeil architectonic frame (by *Antonio Tassi*), a cloud-filled sky is adorned with yet more allegorical figures.

The richly coloured ceiling fresco is by *Bartolomeo Altomonte*; its theme, the marriage of virtue and knowledge, was drawn up personally by Provost Johann Georg Wiesmayr. Presided over by religion, the bond of matrimony is sealed in the presence of faith

and wisdom, whose marriage gifts are a burning heart and a pen – a reference, like many other details of the scene, to the order's patron, St. Augustine. The bridal party is composed of diverse virtues and sciences, intellect banishing ignorance, heresy and other such vices, which tumble vigorously out of the frame. Wiesmayr saw in the life of St. Augustine what he constantly strove to set before his community: the ideal of an indefatigable quest for knowledge combined with a good life.

In 1746 the learned bibliophile sent his thoughts on this subject to the court painter *Daniel Gran*, who approved of the project and prepared a detailed work plan with accompanying sketches. The principal change

Gran suggested was to compose the central vault scene as a single unit rather than in three separate sections. Altomonte himself, who executed the fresco, was allowed very little freedom, as Gran dictated not only the position, appearance and attributes of the allegories, but even the way they were to be lit.

The library holds some 150,000 volumes, among them 800 manuscripts and almost 900 incunabula. The catalogue system was established by the notable foundation librarian Albin Czerny (1821–1900). The oldest item is a 5–6th century papyrus fragment. The first major work of the foundation scriptorium, which reached its peak between 1270 and 1330, is the Romanesque **Great Bible of St. Florian** (1140); measuring 66 by 48 cm, it is regarded as Austria's largest illuminated manuscript. The richly illuminated missals of *Heinrich von Marbach* (c. 1306) and *Heinrich von Walling* (c. 1310), together with the Poor Man's Bible of St. Florian (c. 1310), count as masterpieces of Gothic book art.

Friedrich Buchmayr

Collections

Provost Johann Georg Wiesmayr – portrait from the Prelates' Gallery by Johann Georg Tompke (1753)

On collecting in religious houses

Collecting in religious houses started with liturgical objects that may have been broken and had to be replaced, or no longer appealed to the taste of a new age, but whose sacred status prevented their being simply discarded. Nevertheless, much was lost over the course of time. Only later did the desire grow to gather and preserve works and objets d'art, as well as rarities of nature. This was the initial drive behind the establishment not only of art collections but also of cabinets of wonders. The Renaissance and Baroque eras saw such collections as important **cultural reservoirs**, and various provosts and canons expanded these in line with their individual tastes.

The oldest record of an art collection at St. Florian's dates from the provostship of Leopold Zehetner in the 1620s. In the later 17th century Provost David Fuhrmann set aside a special room for the collection, whose core consisted of late medieval altar paintings, mostly from the collegiate foundation and incorporated parish churches. The systematic collection of paintings dates from his provostship. In 1728 Provost Johann Baptist Födermayr moved the collection to a new art cabinet (today the Altomonte Room), but it was under his successor, Provost Johann Georg Wiesmayr, that it was finally transferred to a purpose-built gallery (today the Baroque Gallery) in 1751. At the same time Wiesmayr equipped the foundation's new library not only with generously purchased books but also with numismatic and scientific objects of interest, making it into what we might today call a multimedia project. The planned four-room technical department de-

Ioannes Georgius Wismayr Austr. Florianensis natus 1695. 4 April electus Præpositus 1732 19 octo. mortuus 9 Julii ſo 1755. Huius Can. Præp.XLI.

voted to the four elements did not, however, come about.

Wiesmayr's intention was fundamentally didactic: the young canons should have a sound general education. His successors as provost extended the natural science collections (minerals, plants, birds, butterflies and beetles), and already in the 18th century St. Florian's could proudly display its treasures to high-ranking visitors and scholars from many disciplines. By 1800, with individual collections under the care of trained specialists from the college of canons, the foundation enjoyed a reputation approximating that of a learned academy.

Karl Rehberger

Art collections

The foundation's valuable **collection of paintings** comprises works from every epoch, either from a liturgical background, from benefactors' gifts, or from the zeal and interests of individual provosts and canons. The masterpieces hang in ten rooms of the former Baroque Prelacy.

A high point of the collection is the almost 100 altar paintings from the

Page 38–39:
Passion of Christ – "Sunday face" of the altar diptych by Albrecht Altdorfer (pre-1518)

15th and 16th centuries. In 1508 Provost Petrus Maurer commissioned the Regensburg artist *Albrecht Altdorfer* to create a large work for the reredos of **St. Sebastian's altar.** The late Gothic multi-panelled diptych was originally placed in a northern side chapel of the basilica, of which we know that its altar was consecrated on April 26, 1509. A box dated 1522 containing the letters of indulgence for this event has been preserved, but the reliquary itself and the carved statuary have been lost. Today St. Florian's has twelve panels, as well as two wings of the predella, from this altar. Completed in 1518, Altdorfer's major sacred work is among the most valuable masterpieces of the late Middle Ages. Paintings by other masters of the Danube School complete the foundation's important Gothic art collection.

The following centuries are represented by many large and small landscapes, still-life flower arrangements and animal paintings, along with portraits and further sacred works, predominantly by Austrian Baroque artists like *Bartolomeo* and *Martino Altomonte* (e.g. sketches for ceiling frescoes), *Michael Wenzel Halbax*, and *Martin Johann Schmidt*, but also including Dutch, Flemish (*Pieter Brueghel the Younger, Joos van Craesbeeck*), and Italian (*Angelo Maria Costa, Canaletto*) masters. Outstanding among more modern works is the extensive collection of paintings, drawings and prints by the Austrian artist *Hans Fronius* (1903–1988).

Completed in 1751, the three rooms of the **Baroque Gallery** hold 230 paintings, hung closely together, in an order established by the Viennese painter and curator *Leopold von Montagna*, who also compiled the first catalogue of the foundation's paintings in 1773. Following the taste of the age, the works are grouped according to purely decorative considerations.

The **sculpture collection** contains two more than life-size wooden figures of St. Florian from the early 14th cen-

Christ Before Pilate – painting by Hans Fronius (1987)

37

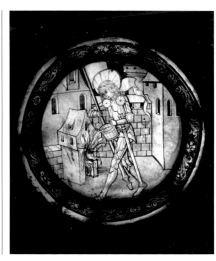

tury that rank as masterpieces of the period. They show the foundation's patron in knightly apparel but not yet furnished with his typical later accoutrements of burning house and water butt. With its detailed depiction of hairstyle, clothing and accessories, the older of the two works (c. 1320) is regarded as a major achievement of Gothic Mannerism. A terracotta Confinement of the Virgin (c. 1370–75) is particularly striking for its unusually natural and tender depiction of the mother-child relationship.

The foundation's remarkable collection of **stained glass** comprises 42 late Gothic items, among them the founder's plaque from the former Charterhouse at Gaming with the portrait of Duke Albrecht II and his family. A Madonna and Child roundel (c. 1290?) may well be the only artwork still extant from the Gothic collegiate church. Also striking is the reworking of graphic art (by *Martin Schongauer* among others) in his male-saint cycles and Passion of Christ (c. 1500).

Graphic art collection

The graphic art collection amounts to some 10,000 sheets, including 750 drawings and 780 woodcuts. The custodian Friedrich Mayer compiled the first catalogue in 1837; this was revised in the 1880s by the Viennese art dealer Josef Bermann (1810–1886), who systematically reordered the collection according to artist and school in the arrangement we have today. Almost half the holdings – which largely consist of illustrations, reproductions, portraits and images of the saints – can be attributed to the German School.

Of particular interest is a group of some 150 Austrian Baroque drawings that includes sketches by *Daniel Gran*, *Martin Johann Schmidt* (known as

oldest item among the academic disputation announcements dates from 1629 (*Lucas Kilian*), and the ex libris collection amounts to some 300 individual examples of that genre. A more recent collection is the 130,000 or so postcards from every corner of the globe – an invaluable pictorial archive for historical and topographical research.

Other collections

The central exhibit in the **applied arts collection** is a group of 29 ivory works. The porcelain collection features a large number of late 18th to mid 19th century pieces from the *Imperial Porcelain Manufactury* in Vienna. The largest single collection anywhere of serpentine tableware consists of thirty 17th and 18th century pieces from Zöblitz (Saxony). The pewter and glass collection is also extensive. The main focus of the archaeological collection is the Greco-Roman period (c. 200 objects), but proto- and early Christian objects are also represented.

The **natural history collections** are kept in fourteen specially designed classicistic cabinets with drawers and showcases. The mineralogical collection (c. 2500 items) fills seven of these, one cabinet holds wooden models of crystals, three hold fossils and stones, and three hold sea and snail shells. Prominent in the collection is a Baroque model mine, probably from the Erz Mountains of Slovakia, bought by Provost Johann Georg Wiesmayr in 1754. Measuring 116 x 78 cm, it is believed to be the largest of its kind. It documents the mining practice of the period from ore extraction and preparation to smelting and the casting of coins.

Purchased in 1802, the conchological (shell) collection mostly stems from the Viennese banker J. F. Van der Nüll (950 species). Other natural history collections (birds, insects, herbarium)

'Kremser Schmidt') and *Martino* as well as *Bartolomeo Altomonte*. Around 250 drawings and sketches from the estate of *Anton Schaller* (1773–1844) – a painter of figures and backgrounds at the Imperial Porcelain Manufactury in Vienna – also found their way to St. Florian.

The print collection contains more than 100 items from the Old German School (*Albrecht Dürer, Albrecht Altdorfer, Hans Holbein*), and the foundation also holds the world's second largest collection of playing cards from the workshop of the Viennese card painter *Hans Forster* (†1584). The

41

were decimated and badly damaged in the course of transportation at the time of the National Socialist confiscation and expropriation of the foundation.

Finally, the botanist and fruit cultivator Canon Josef Schmidberger (1773–1844) developed a method of biological pest control that anticipated the principle of ecological balance which has come to the fore again in our own day.

Friedrich Buchmayr

◼ Archives

The foundation's historical archives comprise some 2400 **parchment documents,** among them the oldest deed of the State of Upper Austria, dated July 20, 1002, with which Emperor Henry II transferred a nearby parcel of land to the foundation. Other notable items include early 12th century deeds of conveyance, and 800 manuscripts, some of them particularly valuable. The **cartulary** (1276–1360) is not only the oldest in Austria, it is also unique in containing not only transcriptions of legal deeds held at St. Florian's, but also coloured portraits of their issuers and recipients.

The **Church Dedication Chronicle** started by the later Provost Einwik Weizlan on the occasion of the dedication of the collegiate church in 1291 related the history of the foundation up to the completion of the Gothic church and listed the many relics held there. The oldest land register, dating from 1378, provides an overall view of the foundation's economic basis at that time.

The account ledgers for the Baroque reconstruction of the foundation are almost completely extant, as are various other account books relating to the administration of the foundation and its manorial holdings at St. Florian, with precise plans of the arable land. The deeds and other documents pertaining to the 33 incorporated parishes give an insight into their religious, legal and economic development.

Canon Jodok Stülz (1799–1872) earned widespread respect for his comprehensive reordering and cataloguing of the foundation's archives in an important reference work, the so-called Repertorium. He was a member of the 19th century group of canons who, led by Franz Kurz (1771–1843), devoted themselves to historical research and writing, and later gained supra-regional significance under the name of the **St. Florian School of History.** Launched in 1805, Kurz's series of publications entitled Beiträge zur Geschichte des Landes ob der Enns (Historical Contributions on the Enns Region) pioneered historiography in Austria based on research into primary sources. As well as Stülz and others, he was followed by Canons Josef Chmel (1798–1858) and Albin Czerny (1821–1900). Seven canons from St. Florian's have been members of the Austrian Academy of Sciences.

Karl Rehberger

Collegiate archivist Franz Kurz – portrait by Leopold Schulz (1827)

Page 44 (top):
Imperial audience room with portraits of rulers

Page 44 (bottom):
Gobelin room

Page 45:
Writing desk in the bishop's room – workshop of cabinetmaker Stefan Jegg (1722)

Noble rooms and central staircase

Faistenberger room
with landscapes by
Josef Faistenberger
(1712–14)

Imperial apartments

The second floor of the west wing contains the so-called **imperial apartments**, a continuous sequence of rooms covering almost 1100 sq m accessed from a small anteroom, the saletta, situated at the centre of the main staircase. Varying in size, the twelve rooms served to accommodate high-ranking guests. They were fitted out between 1698 and 1714 in step with the progress of the building work. In 1728–29 it was decided to reserve the rooms south of the saletta for the personal use of the emperor, so some rebuilding and adaptation of the existing arrangements was necessary, including the creation of a new bedroom for the emperor and empress. Overall, the apartments are a unique example of the domestic interior architecture of the Baroque court, particularly in the festal extravagance of the frescoes and plasterwork on walls and ceilings, the inlaid floors, the panelled and tapestried walls, and the elaborate tiled stoves and chimney pieces. The furniture, paintings, sculptures and wood-carving in these rooms are also of incomparable quality and abundance.

Prince Eugen room with the emperor's bed (1712)

Staircase

Planned by *Carlo Antonio Carlone* and completed in its main elements by 1701, the central stairway, with its double flight of symmetrically opposed steps, stands out against the west front of the Prelates' Court without interrupting the long trajectory of the west wing corridors. In lively contrast to the plain courtyard façade with its even rows of windows, the projecting staircase is faced with bold pilasters and opens to the courtyard in

Page 47:
Main staircase with stairs from first to second floor and wrought-iron screen by Nikolaus Peigine (1730)

Page 48–49:
View of the Marble Hall looking east (built 1718–19, interior furnishings 1723–1732)

a perfectly twinned arcade of mounting pillars. Accessible directly from the front entrance, the staircase provides visitors with an appropriately dignified welcome, leading them up to the prelacy apartments on the first floor and then on to the guest and imperial apartments on the second floor. Work on the staircase was not finished when Carlone died in 1708, so his successor *Jakob Prandtauer* was

able to introduce a number of changes, including the unusual pierced stonework with its fern-like patterns on the upper flights of stairs, and the large central arch that optically links the first and second floors, allowing a direct view through to the stairwell. Prandtauer also used the three central arches of the upper storey to mould the staircase and imperial corridor into a single architectonic unit. He achieved this by removing the dividing screen of Carlone's planned arcade and integrating both spaces – staircase and corridor – under a single ornately decorated ceiling. The result was a work full of southern charm, as Carlone would undoubtedly have wanted it.

Marble Hall

With its mansard roof rising imposingly above an Attic cornice, and its richly decorated inner and outer

Page 51:
Staircase with
Bläserturm above the
main entrance to
Prelates' Court

façades, the Marble Pavilion at the centre of the south wing constitutes not only the architectonic climax of the Prelates' Court but, from the wider perspective of the surrounding landscape, the focal point of the entire foundation complex. Completed in its main structure in 1719 and roofed in 1722, the Pavilion – a major work of *Jakob Prandtauer* – contains the great festal room of the foundation, the so-called Marble Hall. This extends over both upper storeys and takes in the entire width of the building. Beneath it on the ground floor is the somewhat shorter and narrower sala terrena, which faces southwards onto the Prelates' Garden.

The hall takes its name from the red-brown and greyish-white marble (or marbled plasterwork) of its floor and walls, which are divided by pillars and pilasters on tall pedestals that carry the deep unbroken sill of the

ceiling base. Rising above the sill, the tall ceiling with its monumental fresco by *Martino* and *Bartolomeo Altomonte*, together with the tromp l'oeil architectural features by *Ippolito Sconzani*, was completed in 1723–24. The fresco celebrates Emperor Charles VI, enthroned Jupiter-like in the centre, his foot resting on a defeated Turk. Personified as female figures, the reunited lands of Austria and Hungary present palm fronds as a sign of victory. The reference is to the Turkish campaigns of 1716 and 1717, which under Charles VI and his field-marshal Prince Eugen, led to the final liberation of Hungary and the permanent safeguarding of Austria from the Ottoman threat. That the Marble Hall is implicitly dedicated to the glory of the emperor and his general is evident from the large portraits of the two men on horseback that hang proudly above the fireplaces. More than anything else, however, it is the architecture of the hall, with its immense size and festal solemnity, that endows it with its aura of majesty – a sublimity to be found in very few other secular buildings of either the Austrian or the German Baroque.

Sala terrena

Derived from palace architecture, the sala terrena – a garden-room dedicated to recreational summer pursuits – is found for the first time at St. Florian's in a religious house. Already firmly planned into the rebuilding project of 1685, it was built in 1719 by *Jakob Prandtauer*. Its situation on the ground floor of the Marble Pavilion was aided by the southward slope of the land at that point, as the extra height needed for the room could be achieved by sinking the floor level to that of the Prelates' Garden – also designed (in the French manner) by Prandtauer. In its axis of symmetry, the eastern parterre of the garden was

oriented on the central entrance to the sala terrena.

Lit only by five south-facing windows, the room, which has a barrel-vaulted ceiling divided by transverse arches and lunettes, was completed in 1726. The original ceiling and wall plasterwork by *Franz Josef Holzinger*, gaily decorated with Chinoiserie motifs, and the two doorways with their ornate plasterwork and double doors to the sides, have been preserved, but rising damp led to the removal, only a few years after their installation, of the remaining furnishings, including the marble paving and marble wall fountain opposite the entrance. These were used elsewhere. Following more than twenty years' neglect, the sala terrena was repaved in 1751 in plain stone over a layer of rubble. After the closure of the Komödienhaus (in the wing between the two northern courtyards) in 1753, the sala terrena was occasionally used for theatrical performances. Thoroughly refurbished in 2002–2004, it has found a new function appropriate to its architectural rank as a room for festive receptions.

Thomas Korth

St. Florian's musical tradition

The oldest record of the foundation's musical tradition lies in its numerous liturgical books from the **Middle Ages** used at Mass and in the choral chanting of the office. The texts in these books are set to plainsong neumes, the standard medieval musical notation. Dating from the second quarter of the 9th century, the library's manuscript of the Lamentations of Jeremiah, sung in the solemn liturgy of Holy Week, is Austria's oldest text with musical nota-

Marble Hall ceiling fresco – allegory of the victory of Charles VI over the Turks by Martino and Bartolomeo Altomonte (1723–24)

tion – in this case neumes of the St. Gallen tradition.

Church music up to the 15th century at St. Florian's would have been mainly vocal – the first record of the purchase of two organs dates from the time of Provost Kaspar Vorster in 1468. **Choir boys** (pueri cantores), however, have a long tradition at the foundation. A choir school was started immediately after the establishment of the collegiate foundation and restoration of the church in 1071. Still functioning today, the boys' choir of St. Florian's is one of the oldest in the world. Its 50 boys, aged between 9 and 14, receive a solid boarding school education and

Georg Albrechtsberger, he left more than 300 compositions, among them secular operettas that enjoyed popularity throughout the monarchy. The Josephinist era brought considerable restrictions in the whole area of music, and it may have been in connection with these that the entire 16th and 17th century sheet music holdings from the foundation's music archives are lost.

The **first half of the 19th century** was marked by the cultivation of the Kunstlied (art song) and domestic music, and Provosts Michael Ziegler and Michael Arneth added substantially to the holdings of the music archives with first editions of the works of Franz Schubert, who visited the foundation in 1825.

Intimately connected with the foundation during this period is the figure of the important Austrian symphonic composer *Anton Bruckner* (1824–1896). From 1837 to 1840 a choirboy at St. Florian's, he returned in 1845 after training as a teacher, and proceeded not only to teach but also to play the organ – at that time still under the tutelage of the foundation's principal organist Anton Kattinger. Finally from 1850–1855 Bruckner served as provisional organist to the foundation. During his years at St. Florian's he composed a variety of works, among them the Requiem, Missa Solemnis in B minor, and Magnificat, as well as secular songs and choral pieces. Some of these works were dedicated to canons of the community. After his years as cathedral and city-parish organist in Linz, Bruckner was promoted to a double professorship at the Conservatory of the Vienna Society of Music Lovers and at Vienna University. At the same time he held the position of court organist. Despite these responsibilities, he continued to visit St. Florian's, spending free time in what he called his 'holiday room'. And he continued to compose and play the organ on special occasions

musical training. They sing not only at church services but also in frequent national and international concerts.

The **Baroque era** was a high point of both sacred and secular music at St. Florian's. The foundation had its own Baroque theatre, and paid musicians performed alongside the canons. In the 18th century the foundation also employed castrati. On special occasions music was played at table, and high-ranking guests would be greeted with a musical welcome from the Bläserturm, including even the sound of the Hornwerk, an open-air organ. An important composer of the period was Canon *Franz Josef Aumann* (1728–1797), who from 1753 until his death held the office of choirmaster (regens chori). A friend of Johann Michael Haydn, Joseph Haydn's brother, and Johann

like the feast of St. Augustine – or during the Holy Week liturgy he would play the harmonium. Among other works completed at St. Florian's were Bruckner's second symphony in 1872 and fourth symphony in 1874. A lifelong friendship bound him to the regens chori Ignaz Traumihler (1815–1884), to whom he dedicated the motet Os justi (1879). Anton Bruckner was buried in accordance with his wishes in the crypt of the basilica under his beloved organ. His pedal harmonium, used initially for teaching at the Vienna Conservatory, as well as the Ignaz Bösendorfer concert piano he inherited in 1848 from the foundation secretary Franz Sailer, are both in the possession of the foundation.

Canon *Franz Xaver Müller* (1870–1948) continued the musical tradition of Anton Bruckner, whom he had known since 1880 when he began as a choirboy at St. Florian's. Serving first as organist and regens chori, and then from 1922–1943 as director of music at Linz cathedral, he left numerous compositions, among them the Augustinusmesse (Mass of St. Augustine). Among the Austrian composers of the 20th century an important place is held by Canon *Augustinus Franz Kropfreiter* (1936–2003), who also served as organist and regens chori. Known above all as an improviser, he received many awards for his wide-ranging achievement. Among his best known works are the Altdorfer Passion and the Toccata Francese.

The foundation's **music archive** contains more than 5000 items, including many manuscripts and first editions, and is among the most important private collections in Austria. The Bruckner archive contains manuscripts, letters and other documents relating to the life and work of Anton Bruckner.

Klaus Sonnleitner

Provosts of St. Florian's

1.	Hartmann	1071–1099
2.	Isimbert	1099–1120
3.	Dietmar I	1124–1152
4.	Heinrich I	1152–1172
5.	Engelbert I	1172–1202
6.	Otto	1203–1212
7.	Altmann	1213–1223
8.	Bernhard	1224–1240
9.	Dietmar II	1240–1250
10.	Arnold I	1250–1256
11.	Siboto	1257–1258
12.	Arnold II	1258–1271
13.	Konrad	1272–1277
14.	Ulschalk (from Aschach?)	1277–1283
15.	Ulrich von Patnanger (from Enns?)	1283–1295
16.	Einwik Weizlan (from Enns)	1295–1313
17.	Heinrich II von Marbach	1314–1321
18.	Werner von Winkel	1322–1331
19.	Heinrich III von Pibel	1331–1350

20. Johannes I   1350–1354
von Volkerstorf
(from St. Florian)
21. Weigand Mosinger   1354–1372
22. Albert von Rana   1372–1381
23. Peter I   1381
24. Stephan Zainkgraben 1382–1407
25. Jodok I Pernschlag   1407–1417
26. Kaspar I Seisenecker 1417–1436
27. Lukas Fridensteiner   1436–1459
von Maur
28. Johannes II Stieger   1459–1467
29. Kaspar II Vorster   1467–1481
30. Peter II Sieghartner   1481–1483
31. Leonhard Riesen-   1483–1508
schmied (from Lembach)
32. Peter III Maurer   1508–1545
(from St. Florian)
33. Florian Muth   1545–1553
(from St. Florian)
34. Sigmund Pfaffen-   1553–1572
hofer (from St. Florian)

35. Georg I Freuter   1573–1598
(from Coburg, Franconia)
36. Vitus Widmann   1599–1612
37. Leopold I Zehetner 1612–1646
(from St. Florian)
38. Matthias Gotter   1646–1666
(from Kromau,
Bohemia)
39. David Fuhrmann   1667–1689
(from Straubing,
Bavaria)
40. Matthäus I von   1689–1700
Weissenberg
(from Steyr)
41. Franz Klaudius Kröll 1700–1716
(from Wolfsberg,
Carinthia)
42. Johann Baptist III   1716–1732
Födermayr
(from St. Florian)
43. Johann Georg II   1732–1755
Wiesmayr
(from St. Florian)
44. Engelbert II   1755–1766
Hofmann
(from Seittendorf, Silesia)
45. Matthäus II Gogl   1766–1777
(from Donauwörth, Swabia)
46. Leopold II Trulley   1777–1793
(from Fels, Lower Austria)
47. Michael I Ziegler   1793–1823
(from Linz)
48. Michael II Arneth
(from Leopoldschlag) 1823–1854
49. Friedrich Mayer   1854–1858
(from Stockholm, Sweden)
50. Jodok II Stülz   1859–1872
(from Bezau, Vorarlberg)
51. Ferdinand Moser   1872–1901
(from Gmunden)
52. Josef Sailer   1901–1920
(from Linz)
53. Vinzenz Hartl   1920–1944
(from Herzogsdorf)
54. Leopold III Hager   1944–1968
(from St. Gotthard)
55. Johannes IV Zauner 1968–1977
(from Walding)
56. Wilhelm Neuwirth   1977–2005
(from Enns, Linz)
57. Johannes V   2005
Holzinger   ad multos annos
(from Attnang, Vöcklabruck)

Eagle Fountain in
Prelates' Court by
Johann Jakob Sattler
(1757)

304	May 4: In the course of the great persecution of Christians decreed by the Emperor Diocletian, Florianus, the highest administrative official of Ufernoricum and first Christian in Upper Austria to be known by name, suffers martyrdom by drowning. According to tradition, his body was buried by the widow Valeria on the site of the present foundation.
c. 800	Two women, Liutswind and Prunnihil, make gifts to the Sanctuary of St. Florian (ad Sanctum Floriani).
819	September 12: Ellenhart, a deacon from Regensburg completes at St. Florian's (apud sanctum Florianum) a copy of the *Vitae patrum*, a collection of monastic and anchoritic biographies.
823	June 28: St. Florian's is first mentioned as a monastic institution (cellula = small monastery).
888	April 1: St. Florian's is explicitly referred to as a monastery (monasterium) in a deed issued by King Arnulf for Kremsmünster.
907	June 17: King Ludwig IV (the Child) rests at St. Florian's before starting his Hungarian campaign.
1002	July 20: At the wish of Queen Kunigunde, King Heinrich II gives the impoverished monastery of St. Florian's a nearby piece of land of about 30 acres.
1071	June 25: Bishop Altmann of Passau reconstitutes the monastery of St. Florian's and replaces the canons, who had so far lived in accordance with the Canonical Rule of Aachen, with Augustinian canons. Alongside the men's monastery there is a small women's convent, dissolved in the 14th century.
1123	Bishop Hartwig von Regensburg sends canons from the well-reputed St. Florian's community to convert the declining Benedictine monastery at Weltenburg (Bavaria) into a community of Canons Regular.
1202	The oldest seal of the community shows St. Florian as a knight in armour.
1212	Provost Otto, a man of high repute, is appointed provost of Salzburg cathedral, and in 1214 bishop of Gurk. However, he dies before his consecration can take place.
1213	Altmann, a leading legal scholar in what was then Austria, becomes provost. Among his writings are a *Passio Sancti Floriani* and an extensive commentary on the *Song of Songs*, both in verse.
1235	January 4: Bishop Rüdiger of Passau consecrates the Chapel of the Holy Spirit at St. Florian's. Carelessness among his retinue causes a fire that burns down much of the collegiate church during the night.
c. 1250	The vault of the new Gothic church collapses just when the choir has been completed.
1251	December 12: King Ottokar of Bohemia takes up residence at St. Florian's, placing the community under his protection in 1254 and appointing Provost Arnold court chaplain in 1256.

c. 1275	Construction of the new Gothic collegiate church begins.
1289	December 11: Wilbirg of St. Florian's, who has lived 41 years as an anchoress, dies and is buried in a side chapel of the collegiate church.
1291	June 15: Several thousand people attend the consecration of the new collegiate church by Bishop Bernhard of Passau. Due to the crush in the church (it is reported that 11 women were trodden to death), confessions were heard in a nearby meadow.
1295	Einwik Weizlan becomes Provost. As well as writing a *Life of Wilbirg* and a *Church Dedication Chronicle*, he collects all the community's deeds in a cartulary, reorganizes the community's economic basis, and provides the first fresh running water supply.
c. 1310	St. Florian's scriptorium produces lavishly illuminated Gothic manuscripts, among them the *Missal* of the later provost Heinrich von Marbach and the *Biblia Pauperum* (Poor Man's Bible).
c. 1319	Completion of the church tower. Four bells cast in 1318 and 1319 are still in use.
1323	Albert von Gmunden, secretary to Provosts Einwik and Heinrich, brings relics of St. Florian from Cracow.
1419	Episcopal visitation of the foundation and imposition of strict new statutes, soon somewhat relaxed again.
1451	Renewed visitation, again with reforming statutes. No major abuses found. Canon Wolfgang Kerspeck from St. Florian's is a member of the reform committee.
1458	March 12: At the request of Duke Albrecht VI, Pope Pius II grants Provost Lukas and his successors the right to mitre and crozier (pontifical prerogatives) for liturgical use.
1484	March 30: Splayed cross first used as collegiate foundation's coat of arms in a deed issued by Provost Leonhard Riesenschmied.
1493	July 5: Emperor Friedrich III designates the village of St. Florian a market-town.
1514	Emperor Maximilian I visits St. Florian's for a few days and, with papal permission, instigates excavations to find the bones of St. Florian. He repeats his visit in 1517.
1518	The diptych commissioned by Provost Petrus Maurer and painted by Albrecht Altdorfer for the altar of St. Sebastian is set up in a side chapel of the collegiate church.
1534	In view of the religious controversies raging in the country and the aggressive behaviour associated with them, the papal nuncio allows the canons to wear lay clothing outside the foundation.
1569	A prince-bishop's committee regrets that none of the new canons speaks Latin.
1582	Emperor Rudolf II and Archduke Matthias stay at St. Florian's in June, July and October.

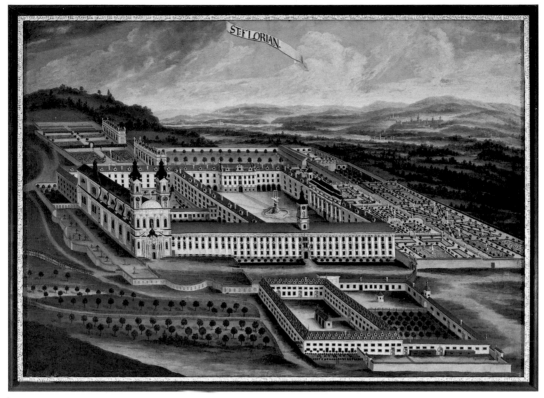

Bird's eye view of St. Florian's Collegiate Foundation from the west by Johann Georg Tompke (1753)

1614	Emperor Matthias stays at St. Florian's from July 25–27 for the solemn burial of his aunt, Queen Catherine I of Poland (†Linz 1572), in the collegiate church.
1624	Provost Leopold I Zehetner begins with the Baroque reconstruction of the old collegiate buildings (today the north wing of Prelates' Court) and of the Gothic collegiate church.
1637	The first library catalogue, compiled by collegiate librarian Wolfgang Rainer, lists 3,946 printed works and 482 manuscripts.
1638	Emperor Ferdinand III appoints Provost Leopold Zehetner imperial counsellor; in 1646 he visits him on his deathbed.
c. 1650	Provost Matthias Gotter establishes a pharmacy at the foundation and purchases valuable majolica containers for medicinal ingredients, as well as medical books.
1676	Construction of the Baroque Meierhof (dairy) is commissioned by Provost David Fuhrmann.
1679	The Collegiate Foundation of St. Florian is accepted into the Lateran Congregation, with numerous privileges. Previous acceptance in 1290 had probably been forgotten.

1684	May 4: After his victory over the Turks near Vienna, Emperor Leopold I undertakes a pilgrimage of thanksgiving to St. Florian's.
1686	August 15: Laying of the foundation stone for the new Baroque collegiate church on the dedicatory Feast of the Assumption of the Virgin. The first architect of the planned Baroque reconstruction of the entire collegiate complex is the Milan master-builder Carlo Antonio Carlone.
1708	October 11: Jakob Prandtauer takes over direction of the building project after the death of Carlone.
1713	July 4: Emperor Charles VI visits his sick queen at St. Florian's.
1715	October 27: Dedication of the new collegiate church by Bishop Ferdinand Raimund von Rabatta of Passau in the provostship of Klaudius Kröll.
1722	A large millstone found during construction work is placed in the crypt next to the stone sarcophagi of Valeria and Wilbirg; it is known as the "millstone of St. Florian".

1726	September 27: Jakob Prandtauer dies. His interim successor, erstwhile site manager Jakob Steinhuber, continues work according to Prandtauer's plans.
1729	Foundation library acquires some 3000 volumes (as a legacy?) from the estate of the Linz lawyer Johann Carl Seyringer.
1730	Foundation theatre built – later rededicated as "Neustöckl" (new floor) and guest-house.
1732	September 27: Emperor Charles VI visits St. Florian's and inspects the new Marble Hall.
1734	List of foundation employees – more than 100 persons on payroll (including 20 musicians), not counting Meierhof and Hohenbrunn.
1736	May 4: Papal Legate Domenico Passionei provides Provost Johann Georg Wiesmayr with a relic of St. Florian from Cracow.
1743	June 26: The imperial couple Maria Theresia and Francis of Lorraine visit St. Florian's.
1744	Provost Johann Georg Wiesmayr employs master-builder Gotthard Hayberger from Steyr to finish work on the foundation buildings.
1751	Completion of the new Baroque foundation after 65 years' building.
1759	Gift of 156 paintings and 3600 books by Baron Wolf Martin Ehrmann von Falkenau und Freyenwörth.
1770 –1774	Franz X. Krismann builds the great organ (Bruckner organ) in the collegiate church.
1771	November 20: The composer Michael Haydn visits St. Florian's with his wife and receives 16 gulden for four days' violin playing. He pays the foundation a second four-day visit in mid-August 1798.
1782	April 23: Visit and overnight stay of Pope Pius VI on his return from meeting Emperor Joseph II.
1784	Planned dissolution of the foundation stopped at last minute.
1788	Silver valued at 35,000 gulden belonging to the church and foundation appropriated by Religionsfonds (state holding fund for former religious assets).
1798	September 4: Archduke Karl visits St. Florian's.
1800, 1805, 1809	French troops requisition all but a few rooms of St. Florian's to accommodate up to 800 officers and their entourages. Imperial apartments used as field hospital. Severe plundering occurs.
1805	Franz Kurz publishes the first volume of his *Beiträge zur Geschichte des Landes ob der Enns* (Historical Contributions on the Enns Region) – a pioneering work of regional historiography based on research into primary source material. Three more volumes follow, the last in 1809.
1807	Emperor Francis I transfers Linz Gymnasium (grammar school) to the teaching and directional care of the canons of St. Florian.

1823	Provost Michael Arneth appointed general director of Upper Austrian secondary education; he seeks to introduce a new teaching curriculum.
1825	May 26 (?): The composer Franz Schubert visits St. Florian's and gives a piano recital.
1826	October: The poet Franz Grillparzer stays at St. Florian's on his way back from Germany.
1831	Stock count at foundation farms: 43 horses, 140 oxen, 154 cows, 24 calves, 98 pigs.
1835	Provost Michael Arneth donates 29 mostly late Gothic paintings and sculptures to the newly founded state museum in Linz; this donation follows that of a large collection of books, coins and prehistoric finds.
1845	September 25: Anton Bruckner appointed as a teacher at St. Florian's.
1846	Provost Michael Arneth establishes a philosophical and theological faculty at St. Florian's; the faculty survives until 1968.
1848	Jodok Stülz participates as an elected member in the Frankfurt National Assembly. Land Discharge Laws dissolve St. Florian fiefdoms; dues hitherto paid to the foundation now go to the state.
1850	February 28: Anton Bruckner provisionally appointed collegiate organist.
1852	Canon (later Provost) Jodok Stülz issues the first volume of his *Urkundenbuch des Landes ob der Enns* (Register of Deeds of the Enns Region); five further volumes follow under his editorship up to 1872.
1874	59 parchment miniatures by Albrecht Altdorfer, illustrating the *Triumphal Procession of the Emperor Maximilian* are sold to the Imperial Court Library in Vienna (now in the graphic collection of the Albertina Museum, Vienna).
1880	April 6: Remains of 6000 corpses (found c. 1290) transferred from the crypt to the burial vault of the collegiate church.
1896	October 15: Burial of Anton Bruckner in the vault of the collegiate church.
1907	July 27: Foundation of the first Austrian Congregation of Canons Regular of the Lateran; Provost Josef Sailer appointed first abbot general.
1926	May 3: Consecration of the new altar of St. Altmann in the crypt.
1929	Provost Vinzenz Hartl establishes a grammar school at St. Florian's.
1941	January 21: Confiscation of the foundation by the Gestapo; canons forced into exile at Pulgarn (Steyregg); provost banished from the Gau (region). November 22: Expropriation by the Reichsgau Oberdonau; buildings leased to the Reichsrundfunkgesellschaft (Broadcasting Company of the Reich), directed by Heinrich Glasmeier.
1945	June 24: Canons return from exile.
1951	September 5: New 20-tonne "Pummerin" bell cast for St. Stephan's Cathedral Vienna by St. Florian bell foundry.
1965	First Upper Austrian art exhibition at St. Florian's: "Art of the Danube School".

Garden Pavilion by Carlo Antonio Carlone (1681–1685)

1971	May 2: Roman decree designates St Florian first patron of the diocese of Linz.
1979	May 15: Choral office henceforth recited in German.
1986	Upper Austrian exhibition on the Baroque world at St. Florian's. In July the Archbishop of Cracow transfers a relic of St. Florian to the foundation.
1992–1996	General restoration of the collegiate church and Bruckner organ.
1996	Upper Austrian exhibition "Living and Posthumous Reputations" at St. Florian's and Mondsee. Focus at St. Florian's on Anton Bruckner (centenary of his death).
1997	September 1: Association of Friends and Benefactors of St. Florian's Choirboys assumes responsibility for the choir school, whose premises are refurbished throughout.
1999	October 27: Feast of the dedication of the church – solemn celebration of the elevation of the collegiate church by Pope John Paul II to the rank of minor basilica.
2000	August 15: New peal of 10 bells installed in the choir.
2002	April 24: Restoration of St. Florian's historically important peal of bells begins with the removal of the south tower bells.
2004	Celebration of 17th centenary of the martyrdom of St. Florian. In a ceremony at the basilica on May 4, State Premier Dr. Josef Pühringer declares St. Florian patron of Upper Austria.
2005	October 16: Opening of the new guest-house in the foundation's renovated "Neustöckl".

Friedrich Buchmayr, Karl Rehberger

Literature

Friedrich Buchmayr, Karl Rehberger, Friedrich Simader: *Die Riesenbibel von St. Florian.* Graz 2008.

Egbert Bernauer, Franz Farnberger: *Die St. Florianer Sängerknaben.* Linz 2007.

Andreas Lindner, Michael Jahn: *Die Musikhandschriften des Augustiner-Chorherrenstifts St. Florian.* 2 vols. Vienna 2005–2007.

Florian 2004 entflammt. Exhibition Catalogue. Enns – Lorch – St. Florian. Linz 2004.

Johannes Ebner, Monika Würthinger (eds.): *Der heilige Florian. Tradition und Botschaft.* Linz 2003.

Karl Rehberger: *Stift St. Florian.* Ried 2000.

Karl Rehberger et al.: *Grosse Orgel in der Stiftskirche St. Florian.* Ried 1998.

Rupert Baumgartner: *Stiftskirche St. Florian.* Ried 1996.

Stiftskirche St. Florian. Raum und Klang zum Lob Gottes und zur Freude der Menschen. St. Florian 1996.

Veronika Birke et al. (eds.): *Die Kunstsammlungen des Augustiner-Chorherrenstiftes St. Florian.* Vienna 1988 (*Topography of Austrian Art*, vol. 48).

Rupert Feuchtmüller, Elisabeth Kovács (eds.): *Welt des Barock.* 2 vols. Linz 1986.

Thomas Korth: *Stift St. Florian. Die Entstehungsgeschichte der barocken Klosteranlage.* Nuremberg 1975.

The older literature (pre 1999), of which only selected works are cited here, is listed comprehensively in: Karl Rehberger, Christiane and Johannes Wunschheim: *Bibliographie zur Geschichte des Stiftes St. Florian.* Linz 2006 (supplementary volume to the *Mitteilungen des Oberösterreichischen Landesarchivs*, vol. 12).

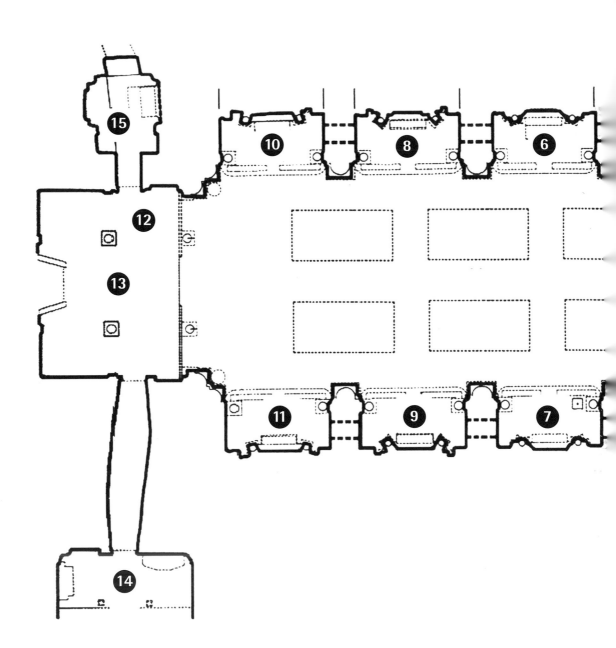